Praying
for
ORANGES

How To Believe For The Impossible

Bible Gateway passage: New International Version. (n.d.). Retrieved January 02, 2021, from https://www.Biblegateway.com

ISBN: 978-0-578-92893-7

Publisher:
The Holy Ghost and Me
P.O. Box 562.
Geismar, Louisiana 70734
https://theholyghostandme.net/

DEDICATION

This book is dedicated to:

- *My parents, who* taught me to live a faith-filled life despite my surrounding situations and never take no for an answer.
- *My baby sister*, who walked the stories in this book out with me as we grew in faith together.
- *My grandmother Leona,* who taught me to fight my battles on my knees and not with my fist.
- *My aunt Ophelia,* who taught me never to be afraid to go after what seemed to be Impossible.
- *My second mom Mrs. Lisa,* who taught me that faith only works if you apply action to it.
- M*y Crazy Faith friends,* who thought I was out of my mind but had the wisdom to follow me even when everything looked outright impossible.
- *My Apostle Leroy Thompson Sr.*, who gave me the foundation I needed to understand my authority and dominion in the spiritual realm.
- *Pastor Ron Walker,* who taught me how to activate my faith and walk in my God-given authority.
- *My Spiritual Mentor Dr. Guthrie,* who continues to teach me to accept wisdom for my sister and insight for my next of kin.
- *My Forever Best Friend,* who continues to encourage me to believe in myself, keep pushing and *Pray for Oranges*.

Writing this book would not have been possible without the encouragement, love, and wisdom each one of these individuals poured into me while I learned how to walk by Faith and not by sight!

ACKNOWLEDGMENTS

My writing coach Kristie F. Gauthreaux who encouraged me to write and publish what God has placed on my heart!

Table of Contents

A Letter From the Author

Dear Reader,

As a little girl, one of my favorite scriptures in the Bible was from Malachi 3:10, which reads:

> *"Bring the whole tithe into the storehouse, that there may be food in my house. Test me in this, says the almighty, and see if I will not throw open the flood gates of heaven and pour out so much blessing that there will not be room enough to store it."*

When reading this scripture for the first time, I must admit I did not read the scripture in its entirety. I only read the sentence that said:

> *"Test me... and see if I will not throw open the flood gates of heaven and pour out so many blessings."*

After reading this scripture, I begin to build my faith by testing God to see if he would do what His word said. As I tried God, my confidence grew, and God always came through for me. As I grew older and began sharing how my faith was growing through testing God, people freaked out and challenged my ideologies. They would swear that my testing God would open the ground and swallow me whole. Little did they know "The man upstairs and me" was tight – like rice on gravy. Eventually, I got tired of hearing their whining and looked up, "testing God," in the Bible. Oh boy, did I laugh. I found many scriptures in the Bible that said: "don't test God," but I did not interpret those scriptures in the same manner in which others previously interpreted them.

I interpreted those scriptures to mean: "don't anger me, don't get on my nerves, don't be a pain in my behind." In MY SCRIPTURE (yes, I said MY - when God gives you a scripture, you should always take ownership of the promise), it translates as, "Ask me for what you want then do what I ask you to do." By proceeding in this manner, you are then testing me. All I need you to do once you begin the process is sit back and watch what I do on your behalf."

The Bible tells us, when we believe God for something, we can expect that He will deliver the promise <u>as it is according to His will and timing</u>. Matthew 6:33 says,

"Seek Him first and His righteousness, then all things will be added to you."

The more we seek God's plans and purposes, asking Him what we can do for Him, and less about what He can do for us, the more we attract His hand of goodness to move on our behalf. Just like any father, He loves it when we spend time with Him - our faith increases as our intimacy grows with God.

Faith is less about getting what we want and more about allowing God to strengthen that muscle called Faith. As we go through multiple challenges, we are strengthened to manage future battles, responsibilities, and the weight of every new spiritual level. To be honest, I still struggle when God tells me to wait but, I have learned that when God asks me to wait, He Is strategically preparing me for future destinies. He Is preparing me to receive His promises for my life.

We serve an amazing Father, who equips us with the spiritual tools we need to walk into the places He has called us to dominate! In my opinion, the word wait is the primary building block for expecting God to move in your life, aka "FAITH." Frankly, you cannot have one without having the other.

Hebrews 11:1 "Faith is the substance of things hoped for and the evidence of things not seen."

Over the years, people have asked me, "How do I keep the faith in the middle of the storms." My response is, "I do not keep the faith. I create it as I need it." You see, I grew up in a *Word of Faith* denominational church and a household with a mom who taught me that faith was all I need to get through the day. Every day, I would test God and tell storms to move out of my way!

This process of matching the promises of God's word to the thing that I was expecting God to manifest became part of my nature. I learned that faith is a spiritual muscle, and the more we exercise that muscle, the stronger we become.

I began exercising my faith muscle at an early age. As I grew spiritually, it became easy to trust God for what His word says. I have continued to test God regardless of other people's opinions - I refuse to take unsolicited Holy Ghost Advice which is the reason my faith has continued to grow.

I wrote this book for two reasons: (1) The Holy Spirit led me to do so - He would not let me sleep until I started writing. (2) I realized people struggle with trusting God and believing He will perform His word! The lack of trust may have originated because of life's challenges. My encouragement for those who find themselves asking God, "Where are you?" and "Why did you let this happen to me?" Develop a lifestyle of Prayer. When you find yourself having pity parties, learn to fight on your knees by *Praying for Oranges*.

STOP LETTING THE DEVIL PUNK YOU OUT OF THE PLACES GOD HAS CALLED YOU TO BE. Sister/Brother, no more pity parties, fight on those knees!

The Bible says that we serve a loving God who will never leave us nor forsake us even amid extreme turmoil: "He has our back." Remember, there is power in the tongue, beauty in tears, purpose in pain, and testimony in a challenge. I pray that the Holy Spirit speaks to you throughout this book and that your faith muscles grow strong.

This book is unique compared to other spiritual books. Use this book to practice faith-building. Be a faith student, do the work to ensure success. This book has a story in every chapter, principles of faith, and activities to increase your confidence in God. Reading and completing faith assignments will strengthen your faith muscle. I believe you can do the work needed to become a strong faith warrior. I pray this book is a blessing to you, and by the end, you fully understand how to *Pray for Oranges.*

Love,

Joy S. Semien

The Little Fish in the Medicine Bottle
Chapter 1

"Truly I tell you, if anyone says to this mountain, 'Go, throw yourself into the sea,' and does not doubt in their heart but believes that what they say will happen, it will be done for them." – Mark 11:23

As children, my mother would make my sister, and I reenact Bible stories. These reenactments helped us to learn how to work the Word of God or implement spiritual concepts in our own life.

One day she was trying to teach my sister and me how to work the principles of faith described in Mark 11:23. She was trying to convince us that we could speak to mountains, and they would move. To illustrate this scripture, she had my sister play the speaker while I played the mountain. As my mom read the scripture, she told my sister to yell, "Move Mountain!" When my sister yelled, "Move!" I had to fall over and roll out of her way. We were around 7 or 8 years old at the time, and we did exactly what my mom said.

From this reenactment, she taught us that regardless of what was in our way that if we had the Word of God, we could move mountains just by using a declaration. The most important takeaway was to understand, **Faith + Declaration = Manifestation**. Although it was a simple illustration, the foundational text helped increase my faith as a little girl.

Fast forward a few weeks later, my little sister came up with the brilliant idea of having a fish as a pet. Specifically, my sister wanted a pet Beta Fish. It is an aggressive but beautiful fish. My mom kept telling her, "No!" My mom believed that my sister would not take care of the fish, becoming my mom's responsibility. After my mom listed all the reasons why my sister could not have a fish, my sister told my mom she would speak to the mountain and tell it to move because she was going to get her fish. Of course, I'm in the background as the big loving sister that I am, rolling my eyes and complaining that she needed to grow up because we cannot always get what we want.

After this conversation took place, my mom said, "Get ready to go to Wal-Mart." While we are at the store, my sister asks, "Can I go look at the fish?" My mom responds, "Okay but remember you are not getting a fish today, Precious!" So, of course, my mom makes me walk with my sister to the fish section. As we walk, I am whining internally, thinking, "why are we doing this?" Mom already said you couldn't have a fish". We finally get to the fish tanks, and of course, my sister proceeds to the Beta Fish; she picks it up and says: "I'm going to ask my mom if we can buy the fish." I asked, "GIRL! Why are you trying to make mom mad today? She already said no." Precious looks at me and says, "Well, I am going to try again, but this time I am going to show her the fish because it is so cute."

So, of course, Precious proceeds to pick up the fish and find our mother. She runs up to mom and says, "Mama, look! Isn't it cute? Can we buy it, please!" My mom looked annoyed and said, "What did I say before we left the house? You are not going to take care of it, so the answer is, no, go put it back." So now I am annoyed because we cannot just leave the fish in the frozen food section. We had to walk back to the fish section! As we are walking back, I look at her and say, "I told you, she was not going to change her mind; now we have to walk it back." My sister looks at me and smiles, and says, "I'm going to get my fish and you going to get one too." I just shrugged my shoulders and said, "Come on, let's go put the fish back before mom gets mad again."

Finally, we leave the store and arrive home. When we get home, my sister helps unloads the groceries out of the family car and then disappears. Little did we know she had snuck into the medicine cabinet and found an old pill bottle. She proceeds to scratch the label off the bottle, fill it with water and place a tiny bead in the water. Then she begins running around the house, shaking the pill bottle, and yelling, "Mom, look, I got a fish!"

My mom chuckled and said, "Yes, you do! But that fish doesn't make a mess."

For weeks, my sister would carry this medicine bottle around the house. Everywhere we went, she would say, "Look at my fish!" She would go up to strangers and ask, "Do you see my fish?" Every week she would clean the water out of the medicine bottle and make sure that my mom was aware that she was taking care of this fake fish. Every morning she would feed the fish and talk to the fish!

Sundays, when we would go to the store, she would make me walk her to the fish section. She would then pick out a Beta fish and tank. She refused to stop. I remember asking her why she kept pretending there was a fish in the pill bottle. I would repeatedly say, "Mom already said no." I remember her laughing and saying, "But mom also said we could speak to the mountains, and right now she's my mountain, and I am telling her to move. I'm going to get my fish". Within a few weeks of my sister doing this, we went to our aunt's house. There was a beautiful fishbowl with aquarium rocks and a small fake fish. Our aunt saw my sister's pill bottle, which she kept claiming to be a fish, and told my sister she could have the bowl and its contents.

My mom reluctantly agreed, and my sister's face just lit up like she already had the fish. We drove home with my sister laughing and yelling, saying, my fish is coming, my fish is coming. When we got home, my sister dumped the medicine bottle contents into the fish tank, filled the fish tank with water, and then placed the fishbowl next to the TV so she could see her fake fish throughout the day. She started the process all over again. She began cleaning the water weekly, feeding the phony fish, and proclaiming that she had a fish.

I remember she would make such a mess in the bathroom. And when I asked what she was doing, she would say, she's taking care of her fish. Then my mom would respond, "You better clean up the fish mess too." It went on for weeks, and she would still visit the beta fish in the stores on our weekly grocery trips. A few months passed, showing people her make-believe fish. We saw a family friend, and Precious began to tell them the story of the pill bottle she carried around and her new fishbowl. Within minutes, the family friend gave her a Beta fish with the bowl and the decorations. The most amazing thing that occurred was that everything she had been looking at in Walmart, my mom's friend gave her that day. She had the Beta fish and all the supplies almost identical to the ones she picked out. Everything she had picked out was now in her hands.

At that point, my mom's mouth fell open, and my eyes grew so wide. I do not even remember my sister asking my mom if she could keep the fish. My sister just politely walked to the car with her new Beta fish and its contents. My sister took such good care of the living Beta fish essentially in the same way she took care of the fake fish in the pill bottle. Not too long after that, I got a goldfish, the very words that my sister spoke!

My sister's active choice to walk out her faith for a Beta fish played a pivotal role in my faith development. After seeing my sister work the Word and produce results, I was ready to do the same. I wanted a video camera, so I decided to do like my sister had done and work the Word. I found a scripture in the Bible and declared every day that I would get a video camera. The scripture that I choose to stand on was Matthew 21:22

"And whatever you ask in prayer, you will receive if you have faith."

I began to walk around the house every day in the same manner my little sister had previously done. I begin to say, "I have a camera." "Do you see my camera," "My camera is nice, huh?" I walked around, professing I had a camera. I honestly convinced myself that the camera had arrived already.

A few months went by, declaring that this manifestation had arrived, and my mom began to ask my sister and me what we wanted for Christmas. I told her I wanted a digital video camera! Unfortunately, she said that she and my father did not have the money to buy a camera for Christmas and that I needed to select a different item. I told her Mark 11:23 says I can move mountains with my declarations, and Matthew 21:22 says whatever I ask, I can have. I continued my spill by saying, "Mountain get out of my way. My camera is on the way." I prophesied my camera was coming! I said it so often that everybody in the house believed it was coming.

When Christmas day came, and I went to the tree to unwrap my presents, I found two video cameras! I started screaming, "ooooohhhhh, Jesus really loves me. I received two video cameras!" My mom later told me the story of my two cameras. She told me that she randomly went into the store and found one camera on sale that fell within her Christmas budget. Soon after buying the first camera, she attended a Christmas party and won the second camera! She told me that my faith produced double manifestations.

Moral of the story: The faith of two little girls, plus the diligence to keep speaking even when we could not see, multiplied by our refusal to take no for an answer, caused mountains to move on our behalf. We were able to move the mountain called "No" out of our way to access our manifestation.

Medicine Bottle Faith Formula

A Moved Mountain = Faith + Perseverance + Declaration ° Refusal to take No

Manifesting Faith in a Medicine Bottle

There are many applicable faith principles in these two stories beyond a fish in a pill bottle and two video cameras. My sister had to show my mom she was ready for the fish. So, she prepared herself by acting like she already had one. She had to see with her spiritual eyes what she was asking for!

Faith + Preparation = Manifestation

Seeing my sister receive what she believed in increased my expectations. Her manifestation came because she worked the Word and made space for God to come in and show His glory! Faith in action is talking it and walking it. So Big Picture – how can the story of a fish in a medicine bottle and a manifested video camera be applied in life? The answer is below.

Faith can move mountains: In the stories told above, our mom was the mountain who told us we could not have the things we believed for. As children, we recognized that our faith was the currency that heaven needed to move mountains on our behalf. Today, regardless of what a situation looks like, we can declare that the results will be for our good and God's glory. We know that we have this authority based on Mark 11:23 because it tells us that we can move mountains!

Ask, and you will receive: My sister and I learned at an early age that faith is about seeing things spiritually before seeing them physically. Like a child to a Father, God is waiting for us to ask him for what we want. We must stop being timid, speak up, and ask God for the things to desire. Matthew 21:22 says: *"And whatever you ask in prayer, you will receive if you have faith."* This scripture gives us permission to pray and expect the promise before we see it physically.

Faith produces possibilities: In the stories told above, my sister and I were willing to believe the impossible, which gave God permission to do the heavenly possible. Regardless of what a situation looks like, expect God to manifest his divine outcome the way he sees fit.

Hebrews 11:8 tells us *that 'faith is the substance of things hoped for and the evidence of things not seen."*

Matthew 19:26 says: *"With man this impossible, but with God all things are possible."*

Together, these two scriptures tell us to find what we believe and believe that God will manifest the promise regardless of how it looks.

Childlike Faith: We were children; we had yet to experience the trials of the world. However, we possessed untainted faith. Go to God like a child expecting Him to perform miracles! Matthew 18:3: *"Truly I tell you, unless you change and become like little children, you will never enter the kingdom of heaven."* To have faith, we must come to the father like children expecting nothing less than the father's best.

Faith is action: Throughout the story, both my sister and I put our faith to work. We prepared for what we believed for, spoke like we already had it, made space for it, and expected it to show up. Do the same thing! Speak it, prepare for it, make space for it, and expect it to show up! Start walking and talking like the battle has been won. Quickly embrace the promise.

"Faith without works is dead." - James 2:14

Practice Manifesting Fishy/Camera Faith

What are you currently believing God for?

How can you apply the principles of the little fish in the medicine bottle to your faith walk?

Do you think you are ready for what you are asking God to manifest in your life?

How can you start preparing for your manifestation today?

What scriptures can you stand on that can serve as the foundation for your faith?

Mommy, Can I Have It?
Chapter **2**

> " Jesus said to him, "If you can believe, all things are possible to him who believes. Immediately the father of the child cried out and said with tears, "Lord, I believe; help my unbelief!" – Mark 9:23-24

My youngest sister is truly a faith force to be reckoned with! She can speak something, and it will manifest. I love watching her because she honestly believes that her faith can move mountains and create valleys. She does not take no for an answer and will throw a spiritual fit declaring that thing into existence. The funny thing is, before you know it, she will have what she said and more. Her strong faith often produces overflow.

I remember when we were children, and the *MGA Entertainment* company released the now-famous *Bratz Doll Head*. It was the doll's head with long hair designed to prepare young girls to be future hairdressers. My sister and I begin to see the advertisement for this doll head all over television and newspaper ads right before the Christmas holidays. Like most kids, we soon became mesmerized by this new toy. When it aired, the commercial made it seem like this was the coolest toy in the world. The commercial showed multiple ethnic versions of the dolls, skin colors, hair length, and body types. The commercial showed how to style the doll's hair and bring it to life in the living room.

Ultimately, we both felt the doll was incredible, and my sister and I both were determined to get this doll! But there was one problem the doll was $60.00 plus tax! So, my sister began begging our parents for this doll, just like she did the fish. When my mom found out how much the doll cost, she was like, no way, that is too expensive for a doll. She then lists all the reasons why we did not need this doll head:

1. We were going to lose all the pieces
2. We were only going to play with the doll head for a little while, and then the doll would end up on the floor
3. It was just too expensive

My sister, of course, was not convinced with her no (she never is), and instead, every day like the fish, she kept pressing for this doll head. She would again go into the store, look for the doll head and bring it to my mother so she could see how awesome the doll was and list all the reasons why she would take care of the doll. On the other hand, I had given up on the doll head and moved onto bigger and better things (that I felt were more reasonably priced)! My mom was adamant about not buying this doll head. Still, she forgot what her youngest child was capable of manifesting. My sister talked about this doll head so much she drove me crazy! So, I came up with a brilliant idea. I would buy the doll head for her, but again I ran into a slight problem, the doll was $60.00!

Being the multi-faceted entrepreneur that I am - I began to do two things. First, I prayed, and then I worked. I learned to work and create businesses at an early age – my dad instilled in my sisters and me that the only person to rely on is God. He would say: everybody else will fail you eventually, so pray and work; that's all you can do. My dad would often say, "Well, you know what to do." This translates to, if you want something bad enough, you will use your God-given skills to create a marketable product. That is precisely what I did: I used my God-given sewing skills to build baby blankets and quilts masterfully. I began to go to the store every week to purchase supplies, make the blankets, and sell them to anyone who would buy them. For a child selling baby blankets, I was pretty good. I sold enough to keep the small business afloat while also contributing to what I like to call "the make sissy shut-up fund."

A few weeks had passed by, and I had saved up $30.00, which was ½ the amount needed to buy this doll, so I was still short, and it was time to go on our weekly grocery trip. I knew I did not have the funds to buy this doll, and yet again, I was going to have to hear my sister's mouth about it. My mom must have felt the same annoyance because she gave us her usual speech before getting out of the car, which my little sister usually ignores.

The speech went a little like this: "Now Joy and Precious we are about to go into this store, we are about to purchase the items on this list, when we get in this store you better not touch anything, break anything, ask for anything, or cry for anything. If you do, when we get back in this car, we will have it out. You both better not embarrass me in this store." Now my mom is a tiny little black woman who meant everything she had just said with the fear of God behind her. This was usually the part where my sister and I would look at each other and smirk because we both knew we were about to get into something- we would just make it a point not to get caught in the act.

As we exited the car, Precious immediately asks my mom if we could go into the toy section. At that moment, I knew what was about to happen. My mom naïvely agreed, thinking that we were just going to play while she shopped. NOPE! Precious headed for that Bratz doll head. When we arrived at the shelf where the dolls were stocked, we quickly learned that the store was selling out and that because Christmas was approaching, they may not have enough in stock to fulfill the demand.

My sister looks at me and says, "We are getting this doll today." Precious picks up the doll and runs around the store looking for our mother. I thought, "Oh boy, here we go again." Of course, she finds my mother, and she says, "Mom, the store is running out of dolls. This is our last chance to buy one." My mom looks at her and says, "Do you not remember what I said before we came into the store." My sister ignored her and continued her rant.

My mother sternly looks at her and says, "Go put the doll back!" As I watch this conversation unfold, I came up with a brilliant plan. I wait until my sister walks out of earshot and says, "Mom, I have been saving my money to buy the doll head for her, but I only have half of the money. Can you pay the rest?" She asks, "You guys really want that doll, huh?" I responded with a loud, "Yes!" She says, "Well, you better take care of it. Find your sister and get the doll." As I ran to tell my sister the great news, my mom yells with a stern smile, "I want my money when you get back!"

I yelled back, "Okay!" I proceeded to find my sister and tell her the great news! When I saw her, she looked slightly discouraged until I told her the news! She was so excited that she ran to the register to purchase the doll. When we got home, she immediately ripped the box apart and started combing the doll's hair and restyling it. She was so happy with this doll. Over 15 years later, my sister has kept that doll, combed her hair, and learned to do more styles than I can count. Today she owns her own company, *Presh Hair co.,* selling hair and other beauty supplies. The Bratz doll grew her passion for doing hair and helped her hone many of her God-given gifts.

As I reflect on this story, I can see the hand of God through this story. In my opinion, God used my little sisters' faith to activate my faith in believing I could buy the doll for her even after my mom said no. God also knew the doll head had a purpose and that it would ignite gifts and talents my sister had yet to discover.   For my sister, God deposited a love for doing hair in her and used the doll head to perfect that gift so she could walk out a part of her purpose.

While my mom nor I could see it at the time, God was using something as simple as a doll head to prepare my little sister for her destiny. My sister's willingness to create manifestations with her words caused her to stretch her faith and be persistent. God used that to provide her a way to develop her skills as a hairdresser and beauty supply retailer.

Moral of the story: Looking back on this event, I'm reminded of the scripture found in Mark 9:23-24, which says, "All things are possible for those who believe" and even when our belief is at 80%, God will help us achieve the extra 20% by his grace. Faith is about believing in the impossible. It's about understanding that anything is possible with God. People are looking for faith moves. There are family members, friends, and strangers silently watching to see God work in you. If you stop believing, who will teach them how to believe in the impossible?

No Moving Faith Formula

Purpose Manifestation = Faith x Tenacity + Patience

Manifesting Faith to Overcome the No of a Mom

This story is full of small faith nuggets or lessons to apply in life. My sister believed she had the doll head before she physically had the doll head. She refused to let up until she physically had the doll head. One of the things I love about my sister is her faith. When she sees something, she wants she goes after it full force, usually declaring that it's already hers.

That is Matthew 21:22,

> *"Whatever you ask for in prayer, you will receive if you have faith."*

Though my sister could not see how it would happen, she knew prayer and nagging my mother long enough would cause manifestation.

My sister had enough faith to believe that the very thing she was praying for would manifest. Ultimately, she knew her faith and trust in God would take her to places she could not access independently. The tenacity that my sister possesses should be the same tenacity that we should have with our Big Daddy God. Yes, I said, Big Daddy God because that is who he is – God is our heavenly father who wants to manifest our dreams as we seek his face.

Hebrews 11:1 reads:

"The fundamental fact of existence is that this trust in God, this faith, is the firm foundation under everything that makes life worth living. It is our handle on what we cannot see. The act of faith is what distinguished our ancestors, set them above the crowd. By faith, we see the world called into existence by God's word, what we created by what we do not see."

Just like Hebrews 11:1 says, when we have a firm foundation in trusting God, then He will create what we cannot yet see! God places a dream in our hearts that He can manifest. We should go full force, thanking Him for what He already said was ours!

The faith key in this story is seeing how God used my sisters' desire to propel her towards her destiny. This faith key illustrates that our dreams as well as desires are placed in us as direct lines to Christ's heart and will in life.

Psalm 37:4 reads:

"Delight yourself in the Lord, and he will give you the desires of your heart."

Break this scripture down by examining it in its entirety. See that our desires are not our own. Still, they belong to Christ. They are deposited into our hearts after we "delight ourselves" in Him, then He manifests those desires so we can walk them out on the earth. In other words, dreams are pieces of God's heart to walk out the earthly purpose He gave. Do not dismiss those dreams because it seems impossible or because you are just plain lazy! Get up and have the same tenacity that my sister had to manifest her dream.

Each one of us has dreams and visions that God wants to manifest through us, whether it is as small as a Bratz doll or as big as salvation for a friend. Whatever it is, God can do it. Remember, if He gives us a desire, He will be the one to manifest that desire. However, we must remember that God is not our personal Burger King - "You cannot have it your way." Like any good father, He wants to know that He can trust His child. Our job is to have enough faith and enough patience to wait until he provides the manna for the manifestation. When God places a desire on the inside of us, we must start thanking Him in advance. Then patiently wait and allow Him to work it out.

While you wait walk out *Hebrews 6:12 w*hich says:

"Thru faith and patience [you will] inherit the promises."

Use faith and patience to see God move. Promise manifestations are for our good and His glory.

Practice Doll Head Manifesting Faith

When is the last time you used your divine authority to create faith manifestations?

Have disappointments caused you to stop believing in something or someone?

Find eight scriptures that reignite your faith to create manifestations. Like a medicine prescription, read these scriptures daily.

1.	5.
2.	6.
3.	7.
4.	8.

Praying for Disney
Chapter **3**

"Truly, I tell you, if you have faith as small as a mustard seed, you can say to this mountain, 'Move from here to there,' and it will move. Nothing will be impossible for you." – Matthew 17:20

My mother taught my sister and me the basic principles of faith. As young girls, we often saw, time after time, how my mom's words led to massive manifestations. She taught us the importance of standing on the Word of God and allowing our heavenly father to manifest areas in our life that seemed impossible. My sister and I would often describe our mom as a force to be reckoned with who never accepts no as an answer. She taught her children this same character trait which has led to consistent manifestations within our own life.

I remember one time, as children, my sister and I wanted to go to Disneyland in California. We had heard amazing stories, and we loved Mickey Mouse, so it seemed like a great idea at the time. So, both my sister and I began to beg our parents to take us to Disneyland. Time after time again, my mother would tell us no and explain that we lacked the finances to visit "The most magical place on earth." In all honesty, she rarely outrightly told us no – her responses were always loaded with faith!

This time she responded by saying, "If you want it, you better go stand on Mark 11:23 and pray about it – otherwise you are not going to obtain the manifestation." Then in her typical response, she began quoting Mark 11:23. It says we can move mountains if we only believe. As she continued her usual faith-filled spill, she told us the mountain we were facing was our finances, so we better tell the mountain to move. She took us to the Bible, and she read us the message translation of Mark 11: 23-25, which reads:

"Jesus was matter-of-fact: "Embrace this God-life. Really embrace it, and nothing will be too much for you. This mountain, for instance: Just say, 'Go jump in the lake'—no shuffling or shillyshallying's—and it's as good as done. That's why I urge you to pray for absolutely everything, ranging from small to large. Include everything as you embrace this God-life, and you'll get God's everything. And when you assume the posture of prayer, remember that it's not all asking. If you have anything against someone, forgive—only then will your heavenly Father be inclined to also wipe your slate clean of sins."

The last thing she said about Disney was, "If you want to go to Disney, every day, stand on this scripture and pray that God will send the money to go." She also used this time to tell us that if we believed God for something, we could not fight with each other or allow strife to come between my little sister and me. She explained that when strife seeps through the cracks, it prevents the hand of God from moving on our behalf. At first, I thought she was just trying to find a way to prevent us from fighting. Later I realized she had a point based on 1 Thessalonians 5:19,

" Do not quench [subdue or be unresponsive to the working and guidance of] the [Holy] Spirit."

My mom also told us to stand on Habakkuk 2:2-3, which reads

"And then God answered: "Write this. Write what you see. Write it out in big block letters so that it can be read on the run. This vision message is a witness pointing to what is coming. It aches for the coming—it can hardly wait! And it does not lie. If it seems slow in coming, wait. It is on its way. It will come right on time."

After instructing us to read this scripture, she sent us to the computer to print out Disneyland and Mickey Mouse pictures, which we placed on our prayer refrigerator. My mom believed in taking whatever she believed for and putting it on the fridge to see it and speak to the picture daily declaring its manifestation. My mom would often say, "If you can see it in the spirit, you can have it in the natural. So, speak and act like you already have it!"

By the time my mom finished preaching to us, we were ready to take our scriptures and the vision (images) and turn them into our daily mantra. Thinking back, I am not convinced my mom really knew what she was getting herself into when she told us to relentlessly declare the expected manifestations.

Every day my sister and I would get up, declaring that we were going to Disneyland. On the way to school, we would thank God that we were going to Disneyland. We started telling our friends and cousins that we were going to Disneyland. At one point, I started saving my money to buy a new suitcase to bring with us on our trip to Disneyland. My sister and I talked about Disney so much someone would have thought my parents had already bought the tickets and set a date. We did this every day for close to a year. The funny thing is that our faith did not meet our reality; He surpassed it!

I will never forget the day my parents walked into the room and told us we were going to Disney. They said, "Girls, your prayers have been answered – we are all going to Disney this summer when school lets out. Your big cousin will be coming along on the trip." They said, "Now give God praise because

He turned the impossible into the possible." I remember my sister and I running around the house screaming, "Thank you, Jesus! Thank You, Jesus! Thank You, Jesus! I remember looking at our prayers on the fridge and saying, "God, you are so awesome. Thank You for manifesting the impossible."

When it was time to leave for Disney - I remember packing my little prophetic suitcase with brand new clothes from K-Mart. It was a prophetic suitcase because it was one of the first items I purchased while we were still praying, confessing, and believing God for the impossible. God answered our prayers, and we were headed to a BIG CITY! When we arrived on our God-ordained adventure - God surpassed our prayers. Not only were we able to go to Disneyland, but we were able to go to Legoland, Hollywood, Universal Studios, the beach, Las Vegas. We saw movie stars and cartoon characters who gave us autographs. We were highly favored throughout the trip.

It was the two-week dream vacation that my sister and I had spoken into existence. I still do not know how the trip came to be. My mom had made it noticeably clear that we did not have the finances to go on the trip. What I do know is that my sister and I combined our faith and spoke into existence what we wanted, and it happened, giving us double for our trouble. Not only did we get to see the manifestations of our prayers, but the overflow was able to hit our cousin, who came on the trip.

Moral of the story: Do not be afraid to ask God for anything. God hears every prayer regardless of how small or how big the prayer. Go to God with a childlike faith expecting Daddy God to hear and move in the only way He knows how. Trust God!

Disney Manifesting Faith Formula

Manifestation = Faith x Prayer + Declaration + Thanksgiving + Preparation

Manifesting Disney Size Faith

Although this story has many faith principles that can be applied to real life, I want to point out six big ones.

1. Prayer changes things!
2. Get a vision and allow God to manifest it!
3. Walk like you already have the promise!
4. Prepare for the promise
5. Expect favor at every turn!
6. Let the overflow fall on those around you!

Prayer changes things: The Bible says in Philippians 4:2-9 to *"pray about everything! Don't worry or be anxious but rather pray about everything."* Prayer is a powerful tool that God has given us to manifest his will on the earth. When we open our mouths to ask God for something, we are essentially activating the dreams, visions, and desires that He has deposited on the inside of us.

In most cases, God is waiting for us to open our mouths and speak those desires aloud. The moment we begin to ask God for something, he hears us, and things began to change. We may not immediately see movement in the physical realm. Still, we must trust that God is moving in the spiritual realm.

In the case of Disney, the moment my mother instructed my sister and me to open our mouths to God, we did. We started praying, we started speaking, and eventually, the doors of heaven opened pouring out a Disney size manifestation!

Get a vision and allow God to manifest it: In this story, my sister and I started collecting images, stuff animals, and anything we could find. We began sticking those things on the prayer refrigerator so we could see them. We began to declare everywhere we went and to anybody who would listen that we were going to Disney. In a short time, we envisioned ourselves to the very place we asked God to take us! When we have a vision, we can see where we are going.

Proverbs 29:18 says: "Where there is no vision, people perish."

Why perish when imagination is the key to manifestation? Start dreaming big and manifest! Do not be afraid to have childlike dreams. When children dream, they dream past impossibilities. They dream God-size dreams!

Walk like you got it: My dad hates when I use the phrase I got because it is not grammatically correct, but he is just going to have to forgive me for this one because I have a point to make. I love watching toddlers mature in their ability to perform activities by themselves because they always say, "I got it!" even when they don't. Here is the thing we must be like a toddler with God and start declaring I got it!

The Bible talks about the children of Israel walking around the city of Jericho for seven days. They marched as if they had already conquered the city. (Joshua 6:1-27). Their enemies thought they were crazy until the wall fell! In this Disney story, my sister and I started walking like we already had tickets to the park. We talked about it, and we acted like it was already done. The Bible says come to the father like a child! It took the faith of two children to drag a whole family to a place they had only dreamt they would be!

Prepare for the promise: One of the critical factors of this story is that my sister and I started preparing even before the promise arrived. We started saving money for new suitcases, clothes, and souvenirs. We never let anything stop us from taking part in our season of preparation. Though we lacked physical evidence of promise manifestation, we had all the spiritual evidence we needed because we knew that the promises in the Bible were yes and amen!

Expect favor at every turn: When we arrived in California, favor followed us with every step. One of the things we wanted as children, was to fill our autograph book with famous people/character signatures. Everywhere we went, there was a famous actor or characters. Sometimes we stood last in line and somehow still ended up first in line. It was like favor was shining on my sister and me in every place we went.

Another time my sister and I saw actors on the beach playing volleyball – we both wanted their autographs, so we prayed to God. "Lord, please let us have favor with them." In a matter of minutes, that prayer manifested, and we were soon telling them we watched them on TV and wanted their autographs. They all stopped playing volleyball and signed our autograph books! My sister and I experienced favor at every turn while on the trip!

The favor of God on us was fascinating! It caused people to stop what they were doing and be good to us! Favor is the scent of God. As children of God, we expected His scent to attract people.

Let the overflow hit those around you: When we prayed our way to California, we were not expecting to walk into overflow. Not only did we pray for ourselves, but God saw fit to provide us with overflow so someone else could come with us. My parents allowed my cousin to go on the trip with us. "God blessed us to be a blessing."

Remember prayer changes things and as things change be sure to bless others with your overflow. Being stingy will limit future manifestations.

Prepare for the promise He has given to you, expect favor at every turn, and let the overflow fall on others.

Practice Manifesting Disney Size Faith

What is a dream do you want to manifest but have not prayed for yet? Write a prayer giving God permission to start moving.

Using your imagination write the vision for your manifestation. (Describe the 4W's: Who, What, When, Where, and Why)!

What are some ways in which you can walk like you already have the promise?

How can you start preparing for the arrival of the promise now?

My Daddy Said I Could Have It
Chapter 4

"Faith without works is dead." James 2:17

I would be amiss if I told you only about the faith my mother instilled in me and failed to mention the role my father played in my faith walk. As a little girl, I was a daddy's girl. Everywhere he went, I would be close behind - he was my best friend. My dad is one of the hardest-working men I have ever known. Ask anyone who knows him, and they will say the same.

As a child, I watched this man tear down entire houses and rebuild them in a matter of days. I have watched him turn old trashy homes and structures into something worth paying a million dollars. He would look at old broken things, see their potential, sketch out a vision, and piece by piece create something incredible. His eye for detail is exquisite. He has a unique talent for constructing homes and buildings that many wished they had. Though he never said it, my dad lived by the scripture found in James 2:17 which reads:

"In the same way, faith by itself, if it is not accompanied by action, is dead."

My dad believed manifesting without putting in work is impossible. One of his favorite phrases to say is, "Do I look like a tree money grows on – you better get to work." He taught us at an early age that we should owe no person anything. If we want something, we better pray about it and work for it! From an early age, I observed my father. I saw firsthand his strong work ethic, wisdom, and love for all four of his girls. Though he is very unconventional and rowdy at times – he is a man of great faith who loves to teach all who will heed his wisdom. While my dad is not without his challenges - when people get to know him, they often fall in love with his charismatic spirit.

As a child, my little sister and I could ask my dad for just about anything. Regardless of what it was or how much it cost, he would likely make it happen. Once we received the item we asked for, he made sure we took care of the item. Like most fathers, he believed in personal responsibility. The more we took care of our blessings the more we built trust with our father, and the more he was willing to continue to give to his girls. The less we worked and the more disrespectful we became, the more consequences we received and the fewer blessings we attracted from his hands! We soon realized this connection and did our best to honor our father.

Like most little girls, my little sister and I would often ask for off-the-wall items like dogs, cats, bunnies, and horses. My mom would always tell us no, we could not have these animals because she did not want to live in a petting zoo. She often assumed that my sister and I would not take care of these animals regardless of how many times we said we would do the work. None of this mattered to my dad – the more we asked, the more we received. Once my dad was satisfied with the idea of getting his little girls what they asked for, he would often sneak the animal or item home before my mom would get off work. He would do this all the time, and though it would annoy my mom in the end, my mom would give in after seeing her happy little girls.

I remember one time my sister and I wanted a horse. We asked for years. My mom would say no without debate, while my dad would ask why we wanted a horse? Without ever having a good reason, we kept pushing to get a horse. Eventually, my sister and I decided to just pray for the horse and expect it to show up! We stood on Mark 11:23 and told my mom's mountain of "Nos" to get out of our way and activate the manifestation of a horse. I started walking around with a miniature plastic horse, declaring that the horse would come sooner than later. I would ask my family, "Do you see my horse? Watch me ride it!" I would comb his mane and feed it fake food like my sister treated the little fish in the bottle.

Within a few months of doing this (I kid you not), my dad came home with a horse. My father told the story that someone randomly found this horse and gave it to him. My dad then thought he should not deny a gift for his praying girls. Just like that, our faith manifested another blessing. For years we had a horse named Lucky, and for the most part, my sister and I took care of him just like we said we would. In all honesty, the horse was more mine than my little sister. She was more of a dog and fish person.

Our Animal faith manifestations would happen repeatedly. My little sister and I would ask for rabbits, ferrets, chickens, pigs, and sometimes before we knew what to ask for, something else would show up. Mostly, it was because someone had given it to my dad, and he accepted it on behalf of his children's prayers.

Years later, we used this same faith manifesting technique to receive a go-kart. To this day, I still am not sure where it came from – we declared that we were going to get a go-kart, and a few months later, someone gave us a go-kart! From these experiences, I learned that if I combine my God-given gifts, with my faith and a bit of hard work, I could produce anything I desired to have according to God's will and timing.

Moral of the story: There is a strong correlation between the willingness of our physical father and our heavenly Father to manifest blessings on our behalf. Like my earthly father was willing to produce manifestations for his children, our heavenly Father is the same way. God is waiting for us to ask for our heart's desires.

Big Daddy Faith Formula

Masterpieces = Gifts + Faith + Hard Work

Manifesting Daddy Faith

I love referring to God as My Big Daddy God in the Sky because, to me, that is who He is. God is my Big Daddy up above, watching over me. I can approach God just like I approach my earthly father and expect to see his hand move on my situation.

Matthew 6:33 explains how to move the hand of God in our life. The scripture reads:

"But seek first his kingdom and his righteousness, and all these things will be given to you as well."

The more we seek to have a relationship with God the more we attract God's hand to move on our behalf. The stronger our relationship with God becomes, the more He knows He can trust us with the promise. If we are not ready to receive the promise God will make us wait because He knows a promise received too early can be used by the enemy to trap us into destruction. The more we build our relationship with God, the more we attract His hand to move on our behalf because He knows he can trust us to do what's right.

To see the hand of God, move, we must:

1. Seek God's face
2. Understand that we are in right standing with God
3. Be obedient.

As promises are manifested, refuse to be like an adulterous woman/man who often forgets their commitments, and running off into the night. When Godly manifestations begin to take fruit in our lives, we must not forget who gave us those manifestations - neglecting our heavenly relationship.

God desires an intimate and continuous relationship with us. We serve a jealous God. He does not like to share that personal relationship - He enjoys intimacy and time to commune in His presence.

Paul found this out the hard way in 2 Corinthians 12:7-10. The Message translation says:

"Because of the extravagance of those revelations, and so I would not get a big head, I was given the gift of a handicap to keep me in constant touch with my limitations. Satan's angel did his best to get me down; what he did was push me to my knees. No danger then of walking around high and mighty! At first, I did not think of it as a gift and begged God to remove it. Three times I did that, and then he told me, My grace is enough; it's all you need. My strength comes into its own in your weakness. Once I heard that I was glad to let it happen. I quit focusing on the handicap and began appreciating the gift. It was a case of Christ's strength moving in on my weakness. Now I take limitations in stride, and with good cheer, these limitations cut me down to size—abuse, accidents, opposition, bad breaks. I just let Christ take over! And so, the weaker I get, the stronger I become."

The Message translation reads:

"Paul prayed three times, asking God to remove this ailment or thorn." God refused each time, saying *"I'm not going to remove this thorn because it is the very thing that keeps you on your knees".*

From this scripture, we can see that God does not always allow us to speak to the mountains, and they move at once. Sometimes we must battle climatic changes as we climb the mountain. It is essential to understand that everything that occurs in our life is for our good and His glory! The delays or the thorns in our lives can be a part of the momentum we need to stay in constant communion with God. One common question we often all ask God at one point in time is, "why did you allow this to happen to me." The truth is that God always has a plan, even when we think His plan sucks. The less we focus on our momentary emotions the more we can focus on our relationship with God, and the more He can reveal more of His plan. Our heavenly Father loves us and wants to see us prosper – understand that there is purpose in everything God allows us to endure.

In recent years, I have learned that God is often working on the "right side" when our situation looks terrible on the "left side". The moment we change our perspectives and focus on the goodness of God, all the pain and hurt that we experienced become almost null and void. There were many times in my life that at the moment, "the situation sucked!" and I found myself asking God "why did you allow this to happen to me? However, by the time I arrive at the other side of the mountain and reflect – I often find myself thanking God for the process. I thank Him for allowing me to walk through those challenging situations because now I am stronger than I was before I started the journey. Remember, faith without works is dead, meaning faith is more than just believing things to happen, but it is the result of constant communion with God. The key to seeing the hand of God move is not just believing but about ensuring that we can be trusted in preparation to obtain the promise.

God wants to bless us, but can He trust us first?

Practice Manifesting Daddy Faith

What have you been afraid to ask your Big Daddy in the Sky for?

Why have you aloud feared to stop you from asking for your manifestation?

If God gave you what you ask for right now, are you prepared to maintain it?

What can you do now to prepare yourself to walk into your manifestation fully?

Can God truly trust you with the promise if he gives it to you right now?

What scriptures indicate that the promise you are waiting on is genuinely for you?

The Walls of Jericho
Chapter **5**

"Jericho was shut up tight as a drum because of the People of Israel: no one going in, no one coming out. God spoke to Joshua, "Look sharp now. I have already given Jericho to you, along with its king and its crack troops. Here is what you are to do: March around the city, all your soldiers. Circle the city once. Repeat this for six days. Have seven priests carry seven ram's horn trumpets in front of the Chest. On the seventh day, march around the city seven times, the priests blowing away on the trumpets. And then, a long blast on the ram's horn—when you hear that, all the people are to shout at the top of their lungs. The city wall will collapse at once. All the people are to enter, every man straight on in." – Joshua 6:1

Another biblical story my mother often encouraged my little sister and me to reenact was the "Wall of Jericho". I vividly remember my mom draping my sister and me with sheets where she then told us we were soldiers for the Lord. She would get boxes, place them in the middle of the floor, and have us walk around it, and declare that the walls were falling! She would then have us write down on a sheet of paper what we were expecting God to do on our behalf. My sister and I would then place the paper on top of the boxes where my mom would encourage us to start marching around the boxes. She had us mimic the exact behavior of the Israelites – marching quietly the first six times and the seventh time letting out a loud shout.

After we did this, she explained the power of trusting God to break down walls in life that prevent us from reaching our manifestations. She said, "Sometimes there is a blockage preventing you from reaching your destination, and it may be way too big for you to manage by yourself." She said, "when you get to that kind of wall, the best thing to do is to keep your mouth shut and eyes on God. Then at the appointed time, shout and give God the victory until the walls fall." My mom's teachings gave me the foundation I needed to believe in the impossible.

The first time I applied faith for the "Walls of Jericho" was in High School. Periodically, I crossed paths with a few rude and condescending teachers. One day after dealing with one of the mean teachers I ran home and told my mom. She waited till after I finished the story and she looked me in my face, then handed me a prayer cloth and a bottle of anointing oil. Her only words at the time were, "You know what to do. Go walk around the wall of Jericho." I knew exactly what she meant by that statement.

When my mom would face a spiritual battle in her life, she would often anoint the physical area and sometimes the person with anointing oil. Anointing oil is a spiritual sign of welcoming God's Holy Presence into a room or on a person. After anointing the entire place, she would silently pray, and just like the story of Jericho, she would let out a loud shout declaring God's favor. Within days those spiritual walls would fall, and she would find herself back at peace. In a sense, she was telling me to do the same thing.

The next day she sent me to school with a bottle of oil, a prayer cloth, and a backpack full of prayers. She said, "now go in that classroom and anoint the desk with oil, keep quiet and pray until the walls fall!" Within a few weeks, the walls fell, and I experienced a great deal of favor from that same teacher who was formerly a pain. This situation occurred several times throughout my tenure as a student, until I realized I no longer needed my mother to tell me how to fight my battles. I began to fight my battles on my knees, growing thicker emotional skin in the process.

The biggest lesson I learned from this experience is that the anointing of God combined with prayer and faith changes things. Prayer is like an airplane, and faith is the gas it needs to take off to heaven. In this case, my mom and I anointed the place with oil, welcoming God's presence and consecrating it to Him. We then built an airplane of prayer and fueled it with faith. When that plane landed in heaven, God and his angels prepared for battle. He wrapped his favor around us and sent his angels to fight the battle on our behalf. The reality is simple, the more we put our faith into Jesus, the more we become anchored in Him, and the more He can move on our behalf.

The next time I applied faith for the "Walls of Jericho" to fall was when I began believing God for a car. Like most teenagers, I wanted a car to drive myself around without being told what to do or how to do it (or at least that is what I thought). At the age of 15, I believed God for a car like the other students in my class. It was an impossible situation because, at the time, my mom had limited funds. During this time, my family went from a two-parent household to a one-parent home. We received government support, were without utilities sometimes, and many days without cash. However, even with the lack of financial security, God constantly came through for us. Knowing my mom could not buy me a car, I began to see the possibility of the situation. I remembered how my sister and I reenacted the story of Jericho.

In this situation, the reenactment of the Jericho walls falling began with a roll of caution tape. I have no idea where the tape came from, but I unraveled the caution tape and marked the space in our driveway where I believed my new car would be parked. I told everybody that came to our house that they could not park in that spot because that is where my car would go. I began declaring it by faith that I had my car, sowing into my pastor, and making declarations that my car was here! I also started buying supplies (i.e., seat covers, key chains, funnels, jumping cables) for my car, preparing myself for its arrival. I refused to let anyone talk me out of it even if they could not see the vision God had placed on my heart.

When I received my license and started driving my mom's car, I would tell everybody that it was my car! Every opportunity I had to declare that I had my car, I would do that. I would prophetically ask my friends, family members, church members, and strangers if they could see my new car. Many of my friends laughed and thought I was crazy because they saw with their physical eyes and not their spiritual eyes. Those who could see with their spiritual eyes helped me birth my manifestation by faith.

I did this every day for four years, I wanted to give up a few times and stop believing. When I wanted to give up, God would always send someone to encourage me to keep the faith. I thought I would be bus riding and hitchhiker for the rest of my life. Towards the end of my sophomore year in college, God blessed me with a 1997 BMW that I paid around $2500 for cash! A few months before I brought the car, there was a break-in at my college apartment. Initially, I was upset about the loss of my personal belongings. However, God used that situation for my good. The insurance money I received to replace my belongings not only covered the stolen items, but I had enough left over to put in my savings account. When the opportunity to purchase the car presented itself, I had the exact amount needed to pay for the vehicle in CASH, not with a loan but with CASH!

Now that's insane faith manifested! Initially, I had no intention of getting a BMW; I only looked at cars I thought I could afford. I limited myself and my God! After getting the car, I felt like the Holy Spirit was saying, "I had to show you what the impossible looked like – you are my child designed for the best." For the next couple of years, I proudly drove this car, giving God the glory for what he had done. What is fascinating is that a few months later, my mom came in a sum of money and was able to buy my sister a car. So now my sister and I both had CASH cars! My faith and the seeds that I had sown into my man of God manifested overflow. As the "Walls of Jericho" began to fall, overflow began to pour out! Though this period was rough, it is the period for which I am most grateful.

While I did not receive my car until four years after I Initially started marching around the "Walls of Jericho", I can honestly say it was worth the wait. Through this experience, God was teaching me to trust Him fully. He taught me that He could make a way out of no way and that regardless of what it looked like, He always had my back. I heard someone say once, "Your greatest rewards are found in the lesson, not the blessing." As God walks us through uncharted territories, we learn to truly trust God and build our faith muscle for the future. Trust God to do the impossible regardless of what it looks like.

During this time God used my faith to increase the faith of others in my life. One of my friends who thought I was crazy ended up receiving her car not too long after my sister and I received our car. This friend once told me that my testimony helped to increase her faith. As a believer we never know who is watching us and we must stay focus and allow God to deliver the promise.

Years later, the doors of overflow were still pouring out blessings on my behalf when my mother and I were blessed with two brand new cars. Unfortunately, a few months later my car was totaled after being hit from behind! While it was terrible, God loved me enough to spare my life and the life of my friend who was a passenger in the car. Not only that, but the money I received from the insurance was enough to cover the totaled car and help me buy a brand-new one. When I bought the now third car, I had to take out a loan – God allowed me to pay the loan off two years earlier than expected with an income of only $1000 a month! It may all seem like a coincidence, but I call this manifested faith! Repeatedly God manifested what I thought was impossible. God will always show up and show out.

Moral of the Story: Believe God through the impossible. DO NOT QUIT! Stick with God! Do not let somebody else's unbelief move you from the places God has called you to be. Trust God to bring His destiny on the scene! Believe that God will manifest the impossible!

Jericho Moving Faith Formula

Walls Falling = Faith x Anointing

Walls Falling^2 = (Faith + Sowing + Favor) x Anointing

Manifesting Jericho Wall Commanding Faith

In life we can feel surrounded by walls as the enemy tries to enclose us with barriers of worry, anxiety, I cant's, insecurities, and impossibilities. We can easily become overwhelmed as he tries to prevent us from entering areas that already belong to us as children of God. We must remember that we can get through those walls and reach our destiny because it is already ours to possess. The enemies' main goal is to entrap us and prevent us from achieving our God-given purpose. The moment we remember that we are children of the Most High God, our BIG DADDY GOD comes to our rescue with His heavenly bulldozer and knocks down every "Wall of Jericho" in our life.

One of my favorite scriptures in the Bible comes out of Matthew 6:25-34. The scripture reads:

"Therefore, I tell you, do not worry about your life, what you will eat or drink, or about your body, what you will wear. Is not life more than food, and the body more than clothes? Look at the birds of the air; they do not sow or reap or store away in barns, and yet your heavenly Father feeds them. Are you not much more valuable than they? Can any one of you, by worrying, add a single hour to your life? "And why do you worry about clothes? See how the flowers of the field grow. They do not labor or spin. Yet I tell you that not even Solomon in all his splendor was dressed like one of these. If that is how God clothes the grass of the field, which is here today and tomorrow is thrown into the fire, will he not much more clothe you—you of little faith? So do not worry, saying, 'What shall we eat?' or 'What shall we drink?' or 'What shall we wear?' For the pagans run after all these things, and your heavenly Father knows that you need them. But seek first his kingdom and his righteousness, and all these things will be given to you as well. Therefore, do not worry about tomorrow, for tomorrow will worry about itself. Each day has enough trouble of its own."

I love this scripture because it simply says DON'T WORRY! Just like God takes care of the birds, He will take care of us. How many times do we worry throughout the day? How many things do we worry about? Is all the worrying necessary? Does it change anything? When we worry, we add bricks to a wall of the enemy, which blocks us from getting to the places God is trying to get us to be! DO NOT LET THE DEVIL PUNK YOU OUT OF YOUR TERRITORIES!

To manifest a Jericho Wall commanding faith, we must first remember we are children of the King! Whether we made it or not, whatever wall is in our way – we have the power to CALL THEM DOWN! Do not call it quits! Break down barriers, open heavy gates, go into the city, and remove the enemy from the throne! We must take our God-given territory by force! My honest advice is, "If you find yourself getting tired, get yourself a friend that has a greater level of crazy faith than you have in this very moment. Allow them to help you keep your hands lifted in prayer!"

Say it with me, I WILL NOT LET THE DEVIL PUNK ME OUT OF THE TERRITORIES GOD HAS ALREADY CALLED ME TO POSSESS! Now, command the "Jericho Walls" to fall in your life, allow God to increase your bulldozer Faith! Look down the barrel of the devils' gun, tell him, get the HELL AWAY, and start declaring and decreeing. Take back your family! Take back your man! Take back your children/grandchildren! Take back your career! Take back your financial security! Take back your Godly wisdom and discernment! Whatever it is, take it back! Break down that "Wall of Jericho"! Tell the devil he messed with the wrong one!

Not today, Satan! Not ever!

Practice Jericho Wall Commanding Faith

What Jericho Walls are in your life right now that need to fall?

What do you need to take back today, and how do you plan on taking it back?

What are some declarations you can use to command the walls to fall?

Check your preparedness level. Are you prepared to receive what you are asking God to manifest?

What do you feel is standing in your way today?

What scriptures in the Bible can you find that make it possible to receive the promises of God?

Snow Speaking Faith
Chapter **6**

"That day when evening came, he said to his disciples, "Let us go over to the other side." Leaving the crowd behind, they took him along, just as he was, in the boat. There were also other boats with him. A furious squall came up, and the waves broke over the boat so that it was nearly swamped. Jesus was in the stern, sleeping on a cushion. The disciples woke him and said to him, "Teacher, don't you care if we drown?" He got up, rebuked the wind, and said to the waves, "Quiet! Be still!" Then the wind died down, and it was completely calm. He said to his disciples, "Why are you so afraid? Do you still have no faith?" They were terrified and asked each other, "Who is this? Even the wind and the waves obey him!" - Mark 4:35-41 NIV

Another one of my favorite Bible stories is the story of Jesus waking up out of his sleep to tell the storm to calm down! I remember the first time I heard this story as a little girl. I knew there was something special about a man named Jesus, waking out of his precious sleep to tell the winds and waves to sit down and rest their nerves (that is the Joy translation). I remember thinking I want that same power to say to the storm to cease.

Well, in 2018, I got my wish to put this scripture into practice when three of my closest friends and I decided to take a trip to New York City! We had the crazy idea to go in December to see the Christmas lights. It was a bad idea! December is one of the coldest months of the year to travel to New York City, and I hate the wintry weather.

Well, to make a long story short, my friends and I decided to travel to the Big Apple as a tourist and sightsee during one of the coldest months of the years. Although it was cold, we ultimately had a wonderful experience seeing New York City during Christmas. Towards the end of the trip, we jointly decided to visit Chinatown because the area has the best food in the entire city! As we exited the below-ground subway, we suddenly realize the weather had changed once we reached the street level. It was SNOWING!

Now, for your knowledge, we are all southern-bred babies. This means that not one of us was equipped to emotionally or physically handle the snow. We were astonished, it was freezing outside, and now it was starting to snow! By this point, we were all highly annoyed and irritated. I, especially, was outright frustrated. While everyone else in the group accepted the snow, I looked up at the heavens and yelled, "God, I know you see me walking here. Stop this snow from falling on my head! It is cold, I can't see, and this is just ridiculous."

All three of my friends looked at me like I had lost my mind. I kid not. All of them, in unison, said, "Joy, stop playing with God." Of course, I yelled at them and said, "No, I am not playing! I have the same power that Jesus had to tell the storm to cease! So, you know what, I'm telling the snow to cease! Now, Jesus, you see me, and I declare this snow will stop falling by the time we finish eating in this restaurant, and we will be able to walk back to our hotel in peace."

My friends started to shake, and they became quiet, as they rolled their beady little eyes behind my head. Honey, I did not care. Now let us fast forward about two hours, we make it to the restaurant, order our food, eat our food, and Joy (that's me) looks out the window and guess what I see! That is right, no SNOW! Oh, when I tell you I just got up and just about started praising in the middle of the restaurant, I looked at them with a smile and said, "BUT GOD! I told all of you it would stop snowing." The look of confusion and disbelief on their face was priceless! They all looked at each other confused. "Oh boy I said. I told y'all my God does not fail me!" The best part of this entire story was that we could walk back to the hotel/slash ride the subway completely snow-free! I danced back to the hotel excited, giving God praise – while they were still in disbelief!

Now, I know what you are thinking that this entire situation is coincidental. While you may be right, I do not believe in coincidence. I believe in God-ordained moments. In all honesty, there are endless ways to reason why the snow stopped. However, there is only one conclusion I choose to accept, which is that God stopped the snow once I opened my mouth out of faith! To be a true faith manifester you must stop calling situations coincidences or overly analyzing solutions to problems you will never know the answer. You must activate your authority to declare and decree a thing expecting It to be so (Job 22:28).

The Bible tells us that we have authorities in the spiritual realm to *"call those things as which are not as though they should be" - Romans 4:17.* My friends accepted the weather because they thought they lacked the power to change the weather. I decided not to take it. God gave me authority over weather. So, I opened my mouth and made a declaration of faith. I told the snow to stop! God used that moment as evidence to help my friends grow in faith and to keep me from freezing.

In essence, my faith connected with God's glory, and the snow stopped falling long enough for us to make it back to the hotel! It was more than a coincidence; God used that moment to show his glory in that situation so that my three non-faith testing friends could grow in their beliefs.

Moral of the story: Refuse to accept what the natural eye sees. Start praying and declaring that a change begins to occur in any situation. Use the God-given authority to activate change in the spiritual realm to change things in the natural. Remember, Hebrews 11:8 says, "Now faith is confidence in what we hope for and assurance about what we do not see (NIV).

Snow Speaking Faith Formula

Manifested Results = (Faith + Action (words)/unbelief) x Authority^2

Manifesting Snow Speaking Faith

Now let us find the big picture in this story. How does this story apply to life? In this simple story of speaking to the snow, my friends initially accepted a season of un-comfortability while I refused! I saw the snow, and I talked to the snow. This ability to change things that seem impossible in the natural connects to the concepts found in chapter one. If there is a mountain in the way, tell it to move! In life, regardless of what is going on, there will be mountains! The authority of Kingdom citizens, based on scripture, permits us to tell whatever is standing in the way to MOVE!

Many Christians go through life just accepting things they feel they cannot change. They pray an "If" prayer that sounds like, "If it is God's will"? That prayer is a trick of the enemy. Praying like *that calls for a visit to the Our Father Prayer* in Matthew 6:9-13. The Our Father Prayer is the foundational script for speaking to God and declaring our need/want. At your leisure, take the time to read the prayer in its entirety. The beginning of the prayer states,

"Your kingdom come; Your will be done, on earth as it is in heaven."

There is a significant difference between saying "If it is His will" and "As it is His will." When we pray with If's, we are not sure that He will do what we ask Him to do, but when we pray with As's, we are declaring that His will is already done. So, from now on when you pray call it done.

Another one of my favorite scriptures in the Bible is Psalm 82:17, which says:

"You are gods, sons of the Highest, all of you; nevertheless, like men you shall die, and fall like any prince."

I love this scripture because, in one sense, God is saying we are a part of Him. We have the same authority and power. Our Father supplies a caveat by telling us not to get it twisted. He is the only God, and we are still man. God is saying, look, I may have given you the authority to call things as though they should be, but I have the last say! Not you! (Joy translation)!

Although He gives us this warning, He still says that we have authority because we are a part of Him. In other words, we are His children on kingdom assignment. Now a question to consider: If God Himself has called us children of His kingdom, does not that mean we have the same self-power that he has to call things as though they should be? Whether it is a sickness in the body, strife in a relationship, financial instability, or anything else the devil uses to distract us from our purpose. The authority to "call into existence the things that do not exist" is our Kingdom right!

Now, do not twist what I am saying. The God we serve is not a Burger King delivering miracles our way. He is almighty, sovereign, and should be respected as such. There are times when God will say no. He will make us wait, but in every response, He considers what we ask of Him. Abraham knew God's faithfulness. Abraham was called the father of many nations, but throughout his lifetime, he and his wife wavered in their faith. Romans 4:17 in The Message Bible says:

"We call Abraham "father" not because he got God's attention by living like a saint, but because God made something out of Abraham when he was a nobody.

Isn't that what we have always read in Scripture, God saying to Abraham, "I set you up as father of many peoples?"

The reality is that Abraham was first named "father" and then became a father because he dared to trust God. God can raise the dead to life, and with a word, make something out of nothing. When everything was hopeless, Abraham believed what God said He would do. He was the father of a multitude of peoples before he became the father of a multitude of peoples. God himself said to him, "You are going to have a big family, Abraham; expect change to come." God told Abraham he would be the father of many nations. Everything looked hopeless, but he set his worries aside and trusted God. When everything looked hopeless, Abraham chooses to believe. He actively decided not to live on what he saw physically but what God said he would do! Abraham trusted his spiritual eyes rather than his physical eyes.

What in your life looks hopeless but can change with a little Snow Speaking Faith?

Practice Manifesting Snow Moving Faith

What snowstorm in your life do you need to stop?

What does the Bible say about your authority to tell the snow to stop?

Write five faith-filled declarations that will command the snow to stop falling.

I Declare...

I Declare...

I Declare...

I Declare...

I Declare...

Now see yourself out of that snowstorm! Start Declaring that God is moving on your behalf!

Praying For Oranges
Chapter 7

"So is my word that goes out from my mouth: It will not return to me empty but will accomplish what I desire and achieve the purpose for which I sent it. – Isaiah 55:11"

A few years ago, as a graduate student, my best friend and I were doing our homework in my office. We were struggling as usual because we both waited till the last minute to do our homework, and of course, the class was in two hours. The worst part of the entire situation was that we were both hungry. It was a bad combination! I mean, who can focus when they are hungry! Suddenly, I had a strange urge for oranges. Do not judge my random cravings. Sometimes we get those crazy cravings we need to fill. That day I had one for oranges. So, I said aloud, "I want some oranges!"

My best friend looks at me and rolls his eyes. He said, "I would like to see that happen. I don't know where you're going to get those from other than the grocery store. Look around. There is not a grocery store near here. I guess you're not going to get those." I looked at him with a smile and simply said, "No, they will show up. Just watch." He proceeded to roll his beady little eyes and say, "I would like to see that happen." I just shrugged my shoulders and said, "Just watch." We continued to go back and forth a bit longer about oranges showing up, and he stayed unconvinced while I stayed steadfast that they would show up!

By the time we finished arguing about oranges, time was running out to finish our homework. At that point, I had to temporarily digress, knowing full well that my God would provide. We finished our homework the best we could. In all honestly, neither of us knew what to do, and we had to be done by 5:00 pm. When we finished, he suggested going across the street to the campus church to an event that could have free food. On a college campus, there is usually an event with free food, you may have to sneak in, but there will always be food somewhere. I agreed to walk across the street, of course – because a girl was hungry – but I was still craving oranges.

As we walked into the building, the pastor greeted us and politely told us that there was no food. He saw the disappointment on our faces. He reached behind the table next to him and said, "Well, for stopping by you guys can take these baggies." Still hungry, we both begrudgingly but thankfully took the two white paper baggies he handed us. I reach into my bag, thinking it was candy, but hoping for something that could satisfy my hunger, I looked down and saw two big oranges!

At this point, I was ecstatic; all I could do was smile and dance. Everybody kind of stopped and looked my way, but I was too busy thanking Jesus for my oranges to care how they perceived me. At that point, my best friend looked at me with his mouth wide open! I could put an orange in his mouth as big as it was gaped open. The only words he could mutter out that big mouth with his non-believing self was, "But how?" And I just danced some more and yelled, "BUT GOD!" He supplies all my needs and answers all my prayers.

I was so excited, and he was so dumbfounded that he even gave me his bag of oranges! That is Isaiah 61:7 *BABY!*

> *"Instead of your shame, you shall have double honor, and instead of confusion, they shall rejoice in their portion. Therefore, in their land, they shall possess double; everlasting joy shall be theirs."*

In the Bible, it says we will receive double for our trouble! At that moment, God surely did stick to that promise! He gave me double for my trouble! Honestly, this miracle is one of my favorite faith stories. I saw firsthand that when I speak, God hears! Not only did God listen to me, but he also gave me double for my trouble! The trouble of having faith even when those around me did not believe! The truth is I had enough faith for the both of us, and those oranges showed up, which is why they manifested!

Moral of the Story: The Bible says if we want something, ask for it, sow for it, and the harvest will come. It is the principle of seedtime and harvest. Throughout the Bible, the authors constantly speak about sowing seeds and reaping a harvest. Sometimes these seeds are monetary, while other times these seeds are actions towards others or even words out of our mouth.

What we put into the ground will come up. When we sow a seed, we must water the seed and wait for it to germinate and take root. That water in the spiritual realm is faith! Faith is the substance of the very thing for which we have hoped. Hebrews 11:1 confirms that by saying like the seed of a plant, whatever we sow, will be reaped. In my case, I wanted oranges, so I took the seed of my words, connected it to the currency of heaven [faith], and produced a blessing. Whereas my amazing best friend [took the knowledge or the reality that there was no store around] and the seed of his word [impossibility] to try and block my blessing. That increased my expectation – I expected God to come through on my behalf. The moral of the story is that when praying for oranges or anything that seems impossible, expect it to show up. God will supply the overflow.

<u>Faith for Oranges Formula</u>

MY ORANGES = Me + Faith

Failed attempt at blocking MY ORANGES =
[Reality/Knowledge] + [Impossibility]

MY ORANGES + HIS ORANGES (AKA a Big Blessing) =
(Me + Faith) x 2(Expectations)

Manifesting Faith for Oranges

Did you pay attention to the story of manifesting faith for oranges? There are many principles of faith. Let us break down these principles. On the surface, there is one person who wanted some oranges and another who could not see the faith opportunity and thought I better buy some. "If you want something, you have to work for it spiritually." Be convinced! Having intentional faith will attract manifestation.

Sometimes in life, people are sent to contaminate our faith and blessings. Still, we must believe wholeheartedly in what God told us He will do. See, I believed wholeheartedly in manifesting oranges, and my oranges showed up. While my best friend did not intend to try and block my blessings, he did not understand my faith level. However, God used that moment to show both of us that He answers prayers, even the smallest ones. There is another principle of faith in this story, the principle of overflow. *Psalm 23 says:*

"God will pour into your cup so much that it will overflow."

Even though my best friend did not believe - he still was able to reap the harvest – then he turned around and sowed his harvest back into me! This brings me to the third principle, Acts 2:34 reads:

"The Lord said to my Lord, "Sit at my right hand until I make your enemies your footstool."

I am not calling my friend an enemy, but I am saying that even if a friend disagrees with us, God has a way of moving them out of the way.

Luke 17:6, illustrates this concept, states:

"If you have faith as small as a mustard seed, you can say to this mulberry tree, 'Be uprooted and planted in the sea,' and it will obey you."

I often find myself falling back on this scripture when I am caught in a storm, and it seems that my world is crumbling right before my eyes. Sometimes life is filled with heartache, pain, loss, trials, and tribulations. Understanding the principles needed to Pray for Oranges can carry anyone through any battle. In a storm I am often reminded of the remarkable capacities of MY FATHER! If He can answer the simple prayer for oranges, I know He is working on my behalf to answer the even bigger prayers.

It takes spiritual maturity to declare in faith the promises of God. When we are too weak spiritually or unequipped with the Word of God, we are unable to fight the darts of enemy when he attacks. When we are weak spiritually, we find ourselves wanting to believe everything will be okay. While our brain tells us, the complete opposite making everything look dark and gloomy. At this point, we must choose to believe and hold on to the promises that belong to us. We cannot give up and watch as everything falls. We must fight.

When I get to a difficult point in the battle, that I feel I cannot manage, I often catch myself and say, "Joy, get up and believe that God can do the impossible. God will always save us from drowning regardless of how high the waves are! Start swimming. God has us in the palm of his hand."

Another version of Luke 17:6 is in Matthew 17:20. The scripture is written in all red, indicating that Jesus is speaking – so we should pay attention. In this scripture, Jesus is specifically talking to his disciples, and he is telling them:

"You don't have enough faith," Jesus told them. "I tell you the truth, if you had faith even as small as a mustard seed, you could say to this mountain, 'Move from here to there,' and it would move. Nothing would be impossible."
Matthew 17:20 New Living Translation (NLT).

The Message translation says:

"Because you're not yet taking God seriously," said Jesus. "The simple truth is that if you had a mere kernel of faith, a poppy seed, say, you would tell this mountain, 'Move!' and it would move. There is nothing you wouldn't be able to tackle."

Imagine standing in Jesus' presence, like the disciples, being scolded for lacking faith. The Bible says God is the author and finisher of our faith! How can we not have enough faith to believe? Well, just like the disciples, we do the same thing. While, the Bible says the Holy Spirit is with us every day, every moment many of us, I included, still struggle with my faith.

We must believe Jeremiah 29:11,

"For I know the plans I have for you," declares the Lord, "plans to prosper you and not to harm you, plans to give you hope and a future."

Know that God has a plan and a purpose for our life. He has plans not to harm us but to give us a future for which we have hoped. Do not be afraid to Pray for Oranges by declaring the word of God - then expect God to answer those prayers. He is a God of His word. Prayer is a powerful weapon that can change situations and cause mountains to move.

Remember that God is always listening and always responding to us. If we want to hear His voice, we must sit still long enough to recognize that He has heard even our smallest prayers. *What are you waiting for go Pray for Oranges and expect them to manifest?*

How to Pray for Oranges

Before moving on to the next chapter, I want to make sure you have the tools you need to Pray for Oranges.

Things to Remember:

1. **Do not be a beggar** – Remember, God does not need our prayers; He already knows the desires of our hearts. The purpose of prayer is to allow us to commune with God. God asks us to pray because He wants an intimate relationship with us, His children. Through that intimate relationship, along with our faith, our request is made known, and we attract the Hand of God to move on our behalf. Remember we serve an omnipotent God.

2. **Do not pray religious prayers** –Talk to God like He is a best friend –accolades are not important to speak with God. Sometimes the greatest blessings come from asking our Father for help.

3. **Listen for God's voice:** Prayer is a <u>conversation</u> between God and us. We do not have to talk all the time, but we do need to listen to God's voice. We must decide to wait for His voice before we move.
   a. God speaks verbally through the spirit.
   b. God speaks through people.
   c. God speaks through open visions and/or dreams.
   d. God speaks nonverbal (i.e., with a sign on the Interstate or a little sparrow).

Steps to Pray for Oranges:

1. **Start by offering praises to God.** Praise is a method of exaltation. In praise, we magnify Him and all that He is! Learn to lift up praises to God like King David in the book of Psalms.

2. **Worship Him.** Worship is a method to acknowledge God's worthiness, celebrating Him for His power and authority in our life! Learn to worship God like Paul and Silas, in Acts 16, as they celebrated God even before He supernaturally released them from their prison sentence.

3. **Give God thanks.** Thanks, is a method to show gratitude. We can offer thanks to God in the same way we would thank a family member or a friend after receiving a gift or service. God is continuously working on our behalf, and he enjoys our gratitude. The book of Psalms provides examples of gratitude that we can offer to our heavenly father.

4. **Pray for others.** When we pray for others, we act as an intercessor going before God - standing in the gap for that person. One of the best examples of intercession in the Bible is when Job prays for his friends, found in Job 42.

5. **Ask God what you can do for Him.** As humans, we

can be selfish and think only about what we want and when we want it. When we come before God, it is important to put aside our selfishness and look for opportunities to be obedient. Whatever our Father in Heaven asks of us we need to do at once! Realize that obedience attracts manifestations. Jonah is a notable example of a man who learned that selfishness and disobedience can delay manifestations.

Ask Him for what you need. Know that when you ask God for what you need, He hears you and is diligently working to deliver the promise according to His will and timing. We know this to be true based on Matthew 7:7-8 which says: *"Ask and it will be given to you; seek and you will find; knock, and the door will be opened to you. For everyone who asks receives; the one who seeks finds; and to the one who knocks, the door will be opened."*

6. **Start thanking him because He is already on the move.** Understand that the moment we begin to Pray that God hears those prayers. In that confidence, we can begin to offer up thanksgiving in expectancy that God Is moving on our behalf! Again, go back to the book of Psalms to find examples of thanksgiving.

7. **Stand against an attack of retaliation from the enemy.** Just like our heavenly Father hears us when we pray the enemy periodically eavesdrops on those

conversations. After we lift up our request to our Father, we should close our prayer by declaring a shield of protection around the promise. This step is imperative to block the devil and his little minions from stopping our prayers and creating strongholds in our lives. Ephesians 6:11-17 and James 4:7 are two scriptures that offer examples of how to stand against the enemy.

8. **Amen!** Closeout the prayer with the word Amen! Which translates to *So Be It*! In closing out with this phrase we are declaring that as the promise is in heaven so it will be here on earth.

9. **Handling Doubt:** When doubt tries to slip in, replace those doubt-filled words with declarations of faith! Remember the devil cannot steal what does not belong to him! Believe that God's words are the only words that matter!

Do not let the devil punk you out of your blessing!

Practice Praying for Oranges

Write out praises to God?

Write out worship phrases that you can offer to God?

Write out all the things for which you are thankful?

Whom do you feel led to pray for today?

Ask God what you can do for him today.

Ask God for what you need.

Rephrase your request into an offering of thanksgiving.

Faith Restored
Chapter **8**

> "Here's what will happen ... God, your God, will restore
> everything you lost; he'll have compassion on you; he'll
> come back and pick up the pieces from all the places
> where you were scattered. No matter how far away you
> end up, God, your God, will get you out of there and bring
> you back to the land your ancestors once possessed. It
> will be yours again. He will give you a good life and make
> you more numerous than your ancestors." –
> Deuteronomy 3:1-6 (Message Bible)

In reaching the concluding chapter of this book, I encourage you not to assume the impacts of these stories as coincidental events. Rather view each story as a manifested faith event. While I recognize that in life, our faith is challenged beyond a *Little Fish in a Medicine Bottle,* we must remember that faith is applicable across multiple situations.

We must be bold enough spiritually to move on our behalf while applying the same basic principles of faith found in Matthew 17:20:

> *"If we have faith [we can] say to [a] mountain, 'Move from here to there,' and it would move. Nothing [will] be impossible."*

Over the years, people have asked me how "I keep the faith and truly expect God to move mountains on my behalf." Well, to be honest, I am not sure that I keep the faith all the time. Like everyone else in the world, I often go through challenging situations, and at times I question God. I have learned that each challenge prepares my faith for the next challenge I will soon face.

The ability to see a challenge as an opportunity to manifest faith did not happen overnight. It came with years of practice, much doubt, and many Prayers for Oranges. There were times I lost faith, and I did not know how to find it. I found myself questioning God, man, and even myself on the outcomes of situations I walked through. While at times I found myself challenging my own belief and faith principles, I always found myself coming back to the very place I left out of fear.

Family Restoration: My earliest memory of God restoring my faith is when my two-parent household changed to a one-parent home. At the time, I did not understand how God could allow the separation to occur and the turmoil that followed. After our household transition to a single-parent home, my strong faith-believing mom was hurt on her job and placed on disability. As a result, financial savings ran out, and before long, we were on food stamps and believing God that He would keep the utilities on. At the same time, my powerhouse-speaking faith baby sister was diagnosed with dyslexia. With that diagnosis came an educational bill of over $10,000 a year. Yet, my mom kept sowing seeds into the local church throughout that entire period, kept praying, and kept telling her girls to keep the faith.

Regardless of what challenges we faced; God always carried us through to the other side. During this challenging season, people paid our utility bill, money came in for my sister's educational needs, and strangers delivered many Christmas gifts. Even when it was time for me to go to college, God worked it out! I obtained scholarships and financial aid. Shout out to my financial aid advisor because without him and his family, I would not have been able to attend my undergraduate institution. Repeatedly, God manifested the little bit of faith that we each had and multiplied it into faith manifested opportunities to see the hand of God move in our life. Those challenges were growing pains that became steppingstones to help us step into and prepare us for future challenges.

Though that season of our life was difficult, I wish very few things were different because, during that time, I learned to recognize faith manifested. What is utterly unique is that while praying to God to move on our behalf, I also prayed for restoration. I prayed that my family would have a wave of peace. I desired peace for my parents, relationship with all my sisters, nieces, nephews, and both of my grandmothers. Today I can honestly say that I have had an opportunity to experience all those things and more.

You see, even when situations look impossible, God can shift everything into possible. For a long time, I only had mustard seed size faith in this area of my life. Still, with every challenge that I faced, my mustard seed size confidence grew into the size of an orange tree, where I began to Pray for Oranges. Over time those oranges manifested, and today I have a loaded orange tree in my family!

Friendship Restoration: In graduate school, I had to ask God to restore my level of faith in Him. God sent me a friend who is now my best friend. For a while, I could not stand him because he would find ways to antagonize me. We would end up in some type of argument.

Eventually, I yielded to this friendship, and I realized there was a biblical purpose in developing a friendship with this person. I ultimately learned that this friendship would teach me about the true meaning of agape, faith, emotional healing, purpose, destiny, and developing a solid relationship with God. I can be a "know it all" at times, so to allow God to use this person in my life to shift my thinking is a big step. Even though he would infuriate me at times, he would also challenge me to be a better person – which is how our friendship grew.

As time went on, we would travel together, visiting places like California, New York City, Miami, Chicago, Bahamas, Vietnam, Thailand, and more. Every place we traveled; we would spread the love of Christ (sometimes unintentionally). On every trip or event, we would attend, there was always someone we would encourage and speak biblical life over. People gravitated to us or more drawn to the Holy Spirit in us. It was utterly amazing to watch the hand of God move through us and help all those we met. It was like the presence of God was always there, creating purpose-filled moments, but where there is a purpose, the devil is trying to come in and break it up. John 10:10 says:

"The thief comes only to steal and kill and destroy. I came that they may have life and have it abundantly. (ESV)"

As children of God, God provides us with a choice to agree with him and choose life or agree with the devil and get what we get. Often, the devil sneaks his little self into our heads and sows tiny thought seeds that are not of God, and if we do not watch it, we will begin to water these seeds, and they will grow into big problems.

The story of my best friend and I prove there will be things under the surface that only God can heal. For a long time, we were inseparable. In his words (not mine), he was the Ying, and I was the Yang - nothing could break us apart. Except for our own buried seeds of insecurities, jealousness, brokenness, hurts, and every other seed that we had allowed the devil to sow in our inner souls. Though invisible under the soil to the naked eye, buried seeds always have a way of resurfacing. These seeds begin to take root and grow like vines that suck the life out of anything with purpose.

In our case, the strong friendship we had become covered in ugly little vines. We had to cut those vines. We had both been through some pretty messed up stuff over the years, and as a result, we took it out on each other. The truth is that we carried the weight of the world on our shoulders. We buried the seeds the devil sowed. We soon reaped the harvest that almost destroyed a friendship that was genuinely God-ordained. Frankly put, we both lacked the supernatural wisdom and guidance needed to be prosperous individuals. If there is a lack of wisdom, there is a lack of fruit of the spirit: love, joy, peace, forbearance, kindness, goodness, faithfulness, gentleness, and self-control.

In my case, my tree was not bearing any fruits because past pain, hurt, and insecurities had taken root and tried to cut off the life of the good seeds. Unintentionally, when we would experience disagreements, I would actively decide to *react* instead of *responding* when problems would occur. Eventually, my continuous decisions to *react* created opportunities for the enemy to move in and contaminate our friendship.

When we *react* out of emotions and feelings, it creates opportunities for the enemy to bring in strife. However, when we choose to *respond*, take in the situation, pray for direction, and move based on God's response, we create opportunities to experience the hand of God.

The final time I *reacted* ended up almost costing me a God-ordained friendship. At the time, I was tired, frustrated, and filled with other people's opinions of who should be in my life. Those same people who offered me unsolicited Holy Ghost advice did not have their life together. Most of them I no longer talk to regularly, if at all. Though I made many mistakes, my biggest mistake in this *reaction* was not listening to the Holy Spirit when he told me to "shut up and wait!" At that moment, I allowed my feelings to move me from the very place I was supposed to be. In other words, I let the devil punk me out of the place I knew I was supposed to be.

Soon after, I felt convicted by the Holy Spirit, who leads me to apologize several times. Unfortunately, I chose to react instead of respond. Because I decided to react instead of respond I did not speak to my best friend for an entire year.

After realizing that my reaction was not a Holy Ghost-led response, I got on my knees daily and started praying for oranges. If there was one thing my life had taught me is that **faith + prayer = results**. It was not an easy year to endure as I watched from a distance how my one reaction cost me a year of friendship and placed both of us in situations we could have avoided.

Now that I look back on everything that happened that year, I often say I am glad it happened because it was an opportunity to increase my faith. Though my faith stood tested, and I knew the enemy was doing everything in his power to end our friendship, I stayed on my knees. The funny thing is that every time I became tired, God would always send me new friends, leaders, counselors, and other people to keep my hands lifted as I prophetically battled for oranges (Exodus 17). Throughout that entire year, I wasted no time. I prayed for wisdom, discernment, direction, and understanding. The more I prayed and followed Christ, the more God was working on my behalf. Eventually, God brought me back to Deuteronomy 3:1-6 and said that restoration was on the horizon if I stayed faithful.

In my mediation time, the Holy Spirit led me to read Jeremiah 33:10, which reads:

"'Give thanks to the Lord of hosts, for the Lord is good, for his steadfast love endures forever!' For I will restore the fortunes of the land as at first, says the Lord."

As I read these two scriptures, I knew that God showed me that He was working on my request. I prayed and prophesied that God would restore, redeem, beautify, unify, complete, and finalize the situation. His will, not my own. I fell in love with these two scriptures and began to connect my prayers for oranges and my faith to these two scriptures.

As I stayed in communion with God, He brought me to Matthew 6:33, which reads:

"Seek first the kingdom of God and his righteousness, and all these things will be added to you."

In this scripture, I learned that the more time I spent seeking God, the less time I had to worry about my mediocre problems. The more I feared, the more anxiety would creep up in my life and try to strangle the life out of me. The more I yielded to the Holy Spirit, the less I even cared about what was going on around me. In my heart, I believed God was going to restore, even when longtime friends told me to let it go, even when my thoughts would say this was a waste of time. Still, I knew that I had to do what God asked me to do to get there.

Throughout the entire year, I choose to Pray for Oranges and be obedient. Whatever God asked me to do, I did it – no questions asked! Wherever He asked me to serve, I served-no questions asked. Eventually, God led me to:

- Establish a virtual Bible study for girls all over the nation
- Establish a virtual tutoring company to support parents affected by the COVID-19 Pandemic
- Establish a virtual training company designed to supply online classes to companies who cannot physically be together because of the COVID-19 pandemic.
- Establish a ministry crossover that teaches people to establish a relationship with God. The crossover touches people all over the world through podcasting, vlogging, and blogging.
- God even led me to write books like this one.

The reality is that the more I prayed for oranges and activated my faith through sowing, serving, and confessions, I watched the hand of God release restoration. My obedience produced manifestation, and God restored the friendship just like he said He would. While I was actively waiting for God to work in one area, He had me working in a different area producing kingdom-minded businesses and opportunities.

In one of my whining sessions with the Holy Spirit, God said, "I do not need your help to do what I already promised – get out of the way and do what I told you to do." After hearing this spiritual prompting, I decided to commit to the works of the Father. Realizing that God only requires our obedience. At times, our worry and stress can get in the way of God working on our behalf, which is why He tells us to "sit down and rest our nerves," like my mom used to say.

In Genesis 2:1, God puts the man (Adam) to sleep while removing one of his ribs to create his companion Eve. I believe the reason God placed Adam under Heavenly anesthesia was so Adam could stay out of "God's business." If Adam were awake while God was creating Eve, he would have probably been "all up in God's business." Can you imagine what Adam would have said to God? I picture him saying something like this: "God make sure her hips have the right curves. Make sure she has long dark hair, and make sure she is not cross-eyed. Make sure she does not talk back." He may have even tried to tell God which rib to take out, and the list of possibilities can go on and on.

Like Adam, sometimes God must put us under heavenly anesthesia to keep us from interfering with His plans. When we realize that God has everything under control, the freer, we will be. We give God the freedom to do what He does best, create opportunities for faith manifested. The more God kept me busy, the more I saw Him answer my prayers for oranges. So much so when God would tell me to do something, and orange would randomly appear.

I guess you could say I was like Gideon in the Bible – God was constantly sending me signs to say I hear you, Joy, but keep moving. The more oranges I saw, the more convinced I became, but the fewer oranges I saw, the more I prayed. Eventually, God worked everything out, and my prayer for oranges manifested into restoration.

When you Pray for Oranges be in expectancy for their arrival! God hears your every prayer.

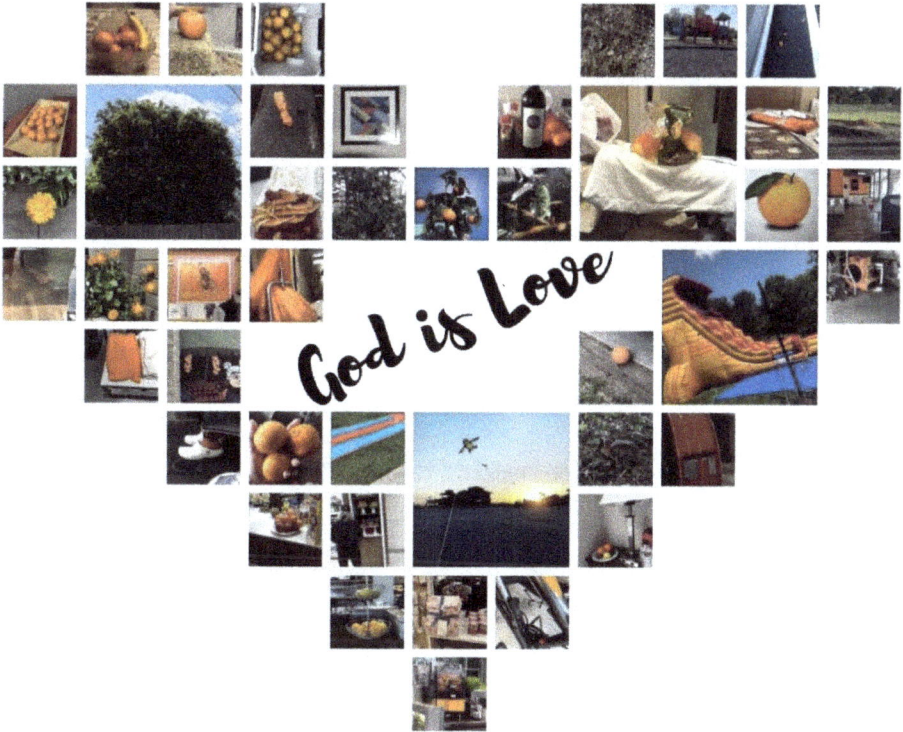

God is Love

Be prepared to hear His response, do not be too busy talking or worrying that you miss His response to your prayers.

Pray for Oranges and Expect Oranges to arrive!

Moral of the story: Whatever we believe for, we cannot stop. Faith can open doors other people say are locked. Whatever God tells us to do, we must do it! No matter how a situation looks – DO NOT GIVE UP because there is purpose in pain. "DO NOT LET THE DEVIL PUNK YOU OUT OF THE PLACES GOD HAS CALLED YOU TO BE!" The more we yield to God and move in obedience, the more we will attract God's hands to our situation. Keep praying for oranges and expect the harvest soon. Remember, we are closer than we think we are evidence of kingdom manifestation.

Faith Restored Formula

Faith Restored =
Faith + Praying for Oranges + Obedience

Manifesting Restored Faith

God hears every prayer we pray, and He moves the moment we open our mouths (sometimes before then). Initially, as I walked through this situation, I did not realize that I was standing in a faith manifested moment. In other words, what I considered as impossible was God's opportunity to create possibilities.

One of the biggest lessons I learned during this period is that God needs my faith active as well as a willing and obedient heart. One of my favorite restoration scriptures that was introduced to me, by the Holy Spirit, during these periods was Deuteronomy 3:1-7, which reads:

"God, your God, will restore everything you lost; he'll have compassion on you; he'll come back and pick up the pieces from all the places where you were scattered. No matter how far away you end up, God, your God, will get you out of there and bring you back to the land your ancestors once possessed. It will be yours again. He will give you a good life and make you more numerous than your ancestors. God, your God, will cut away the thick calluses on your heart and your children's hearts, freeing you to love God, your God, with your whole heart and soul and live, really live."

Through this scripture, the Holy Spirit deposited into me that he is capable of:

1. Restoring whatever is lost
2. He offers compassion
3. He will pick up the pieces
4. He will bring you back from where you are scattered
5. He will cut away the thick calluses of your heart

Now for all those overly analytical people who may have thought the stories in this book were coincidental – let me assure you that this story was not. The door to our friendship was tight. There was not enough space for an ant to crawl through it. Time and time again, when I would go back to my friend, I would hear the words "no," "it's too late," "it is what it," or "we had what we had." I was under the impression he could care less about me. However, the more I heard those words and tried to let go, the more I felt the Holy Spirit say, "try it again". Regardless of what was said to me, I kept praying for oranges, stayed on my knees. I allowed God to reveal scriptures to me, I wrote declarations, and I moved in obedience! A year later, God turned a locked door into an unlocked and opened door restoring the friendship.

Today I thank God for his faithfulness and his ability to honor his promises. I learned many lessons over that year, but the biggest lesson I learned was to expect the harvest when I Pray for Oranges.

Practice Praying for Restoration

What would you like God to restore in your life?

Why do you want God to restore that thing/area/person? Is the thing/area/person that you are praying for restoration adding value or subtracting value from your life?

Pray about the purpose of restoration. Ask God to give you a vision for restoration once you receive your answer. Use this space to write down their revealed purpose in your life.

If God restores that thing/area/person in your life, are you ready (prepared) to receive it?

CONCLUSION

I fell in love with God at an early age. Though my faith has wavered over the years, I have learned that the key to manifested belief is believing, seeking God's face, and moving when God tells us to move. In all honesty, now I love talking to God. Spending time in the Word and communing with God is amazing. Remember connecting with God attracts the hand of God. He will move on our behalf.

Remember, there is a difference between religion and a relationship. Religion is full of protocols, while a relationship forms through intimate communion that produces direction and wisdom for what is to come. Commune with God to see His providence in every area that seems barren. All He needs is our prayers and our willingness to be obedient.

A while back, I heard a message by Pastor Michael Todd called "crazy faith." During that message, Pastor Todd spoke about "How God gave him a vision for their church, they would move into a facility that seemed impossible. God told him that if he stayed faithful, he would see the manifestations of that vision. (If you have not heard the message, you are missing a powerful Word– go to YouTube Today and check it out!). I did not realize God had given me more crazy faith visions and manifestations than I can count until that moment. Every story in this book embodies that principle of crazy faith. Crazy faith is believing in the impossible and expecting God to create possibilities.

To see crazy faith manifested in your life, make a point today and every day to actively commune with God and establish a real relationship with Him.

Faith Formulas

Faith Formulas		
Name	**Formula/Equation**	**Intended Results**
Medicine Bottle Faith	Faith + Perseverance + declaration * Refusal to take No	= A Moved Mountain
No Moving Faith	Faith x Tenacity + Patience	= Purpose Manifestation
Disney Faith	Faith x Prayer + Declaration + Thanksgiving + Preparation	= Manifestation
Big Daddy Faith	Gifts + Faith + Hard Work	= Masterpieces
Jericho Moving Faith	Faith x Anointing	= Walls Falling
	(Faith + Sowing + Favor) x Anointing	= Walls Falling 2
Snow Speaking Faith	(Faith + Action (words)/unbelief) x Authority2	= Manifested Results
Faith for Oranges	[Me] + [Faith]	= My Oranges
	[Reality/Knowledge] + [Impossibility]	= Failed attempt at blocking My Oranges
	Me] + [Faith]) * 2 [Expectation]	= My Oranges + His Oranges (AKA a Really Big Blessing)
Faith Restored	Faith + Praying for Oranges + Obedience	= Faith Restored

When Life tries to buck you off its back like an angry bull, strap up, grab an orange off the victory tree and pray! Use your faith formulas to activate His manifestations in your life! Remember you are in God's hands and the victory has already been won!

Illustration by: Designs by Faith
https://faiththecreatorr.com/

SINNERS PRAYER

Here is the sinner's prayer. It is a prayer that guides you in establishing your relationship with God if you have not already done.

Dear God,

Today I surrender my life to You. I know that I may miss the target sometimes and do not get everything right. I realize that I cannot do anything without you, and I am tired of trying.

Today, I ask that you come into my life and save me. Teach me to be more like you and walk in your way.

Today I accept your son Jesus to live on the inside of me. I ask that you teach me to walk like Christ in all that I do. Transform my heart and my soul as I commit my life to you.

In Jesus' name, I pray, Amen!

ABOUT THE AUTHOR

Joy Semien is an award-winning author and presenter. She holds a Bachelor of Science degree from Dillard University (2015) in Biology with a minor in Chemistry. Joy has a master's degree from Texas Southern University (2017) in Urban Planning and Environmental Policy. She also holds a ministerial diploma from Ever Increasing Word Training Center (2017) under the leadership of Apostle Leroy Thompson.

In 2020, Joy founded The Holy Ghost and Me ministry crossover. The crossover is a subsidiary of L.E.E.D. With Joy LLC. Listening, Engaging, Empowering, and Driving Change. Through the crossover, Joy seeks to teach people how to establish a solid relationship with the one who made them (GOD) through regular blogging, vlogging, and podcasting.

To learn more about Joy and L.E.E.D. With Joy, visit https://leedingwithjoy.com. To learn more about The Holy Ghost and Me, visit the website https://theholyghostandme.net, follow @theholyghostandme on Instagram, Facebook, and YouTube.

Additional Book(s) by the Author: The Holy Ghost and Me